MY STORY TIME.

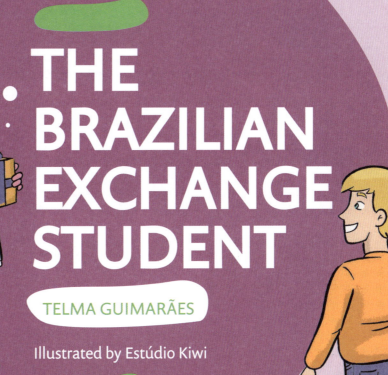

THE BRAZILIAN EXCHANGE STUDENT

TELMA GUIMARÃES

Illustrated by Estúdio Kiwi

Daniel is an exchange student from Brazil. He is now living with Jim and Letitia George in Lake City, South Carolina.

His American brothers are Jeremy and Timothy. Jeremy is thirteen and Tim is fifteen, the same age as Daniel.

They all have lunch at the school cafeteria. Classes begin at seven in the morning and end at four in the afternoon. When they have gym classes, the girls are always around to watch them.

Daniel was afraid to be left out but his brothers introduced him to a lot of people. At first, he didn't know his classmates' names but he learned quickly.

Daniel thinks American breakfasts are much better than Brazilian breakfasts. They have scrambled eggs, toast, butter, bagels, cereal and milk, and waffles and syrup.

Tim told Daniel that Jeremy used to have a girlfriend but they broke up a few weeks ago. She's their next-door neighbor but Daniel hasn't met her yet.

"Hi! If you need some help, just let me know," a beautiful girl said as she stopped by Daniel's table. She smiled at him. "I live next door to you and I saw you when you went in with your suitcases last Saturday. In fact, I helped your host family with the welcome banner."

Daniel was going to thank her for the offer and ask her name but suddenly the school bell rang and he had to go to his next class. Other students were friendly, too.

On the bus, going home from school, one of Daniel's brothers teased him and said "Hi there, Brazilian boy! The girls seem to like you!"

The first week at school wasn't so bad. Daniel was a freshman and had already made a few friends and improved his English a little. He had also met the most beautiful girl he had ever seen in his life, did a lot of homework, and a lot of laundry, too.

It was almost Christmas and he missed his family.

"Danny, would you help us with the Christmas tree?" Letitia asked him.

He had never decorated a tree before, but he joined in the Christmas spirit. There were lots of presents under the tree and he thought it would be nice to put his there, too.

It was very cold, but the fire in the fireplace was nice and warm and everybody was singing Christmas carols, except his two brothers, who were arguing, just like Daniel did in Brazil.

On Christmas Eve someone suddenly rang the doorbell.

Some neighbors had stopped by for a visit and Daniel's mom opened the door for them.

"Come on in, Barry. Come in, Ruth. Oh, Liddy, you look terrific! Merry Christmas to you all!"

"Merry Christmas!" they all said.

Letitia was right. The girl's parents looked pretty cool. And Liddy, the girl that spoke to Daniel in the cafeteria, was really something.

While the women were setting the dinner table, Daniel and Liddy sat near the fireplace. Jeremy paid attention to the couple, but he also kept on watching TV. The men started talking about the money market and Tim seemed to be absolutely fascinated with Liddy. She had long blonde hair, blue eyes, was wearing a blue sweater, jeans, boots and was wearing some perfume he had never smelled before.

Then Daniel remembered the first night with his brother. Tim had told him he was in love with his neighbor but they had broken up!

"Oh, so we are interested in the same girl," Daniel thought. Daniel was a foreigner, with dark eyes, brown hair, a heavy Brazilian accent and still making many mistakes in English. His "brother" had fallen in love first. He would be the second in line or even after the whole school, he supposed.

Christmas Eve dinner was delicious.

The telephone rang. It was Daniel's parents from Brazil.

"Look, it's snowing again!" someone shouted and everyone stood up and went outside as he hung up the phone.

"This is only the second time I've seen snow," he exclaimed. It had snowed the day before and he spent a lot of time playing outside. He felt like a child.

The adults went back into the house and so did his brothers.

He was freezing but his heart was burning. There was Liddy and the snow. The rest was silence.

"Do you want to make a snowman?" she asked Daniel.

"Sure! It will be my first one," he said.

"I liked it when I heard you talking in your native language on the phone. Portuguese, isn't it?" She was wearing gloves to protect her hands from the cold.

"I thought you would say Spanish!" Daniel said as he helped her with the snowman.

"I like geography, Danny. I know where South America is and the name of Brazil's capital, Brasília," she said in a heavy American accent in Portuguese.

"You're smart, and different from the other girls." Daniel felt his heart beating harder.

"And I like the way you speak English. It's cute," she said, as she picked up a shovel near a tree.

"You're... beautiful!" he added.

As they made the snowman they went on talking about things they had in common, like movies, actors, actresses, games and more. They had a lot in common, even though they were from different countries,

"We need a carrot for its nose." Liddy said as she stood up and went in to find one.

Daniel had been feeling happy until he saw Tim looking at him through a bedroom window. Tim looked unhappy.

It wasn't fair. Tim, was in love with the girl that Daniel was with, outside. Daniel was having fun making the snowman, talking and falling in love with her.

"Hey, Brazil, can you hear me?" Liddy had brought an old hat and a handkerchief to put on the snowman.

"Yes, I was just thinking..." Daniel started to say.

"About what? Thinking about a Brazilian girlfriend?" she asked with a laugh.

"Yes. We broke up..." was all he could say.

"I broke up with my boyfriend, too," she said as she looked him in the eyes.

"I'd have a chance with the girl of my dreams! Daniel, this isn't right! Tim loves her and he knew her first. If you're living with his family you should respect your brother's feelings." Daniel thought and felt ashamed.

"Would you like to go to a party with me?" Liddy asked Daniel

"I don't know." Daniel answered. He was freezing and confused.

Liddy went on making the snowman. "We're going to have a party at my house on the thirtieth," she said. "If you want to come, let me know." She seemed annoyed with his doubt.

Liddy put the hat on the snowman and Daniel added the carrot. They had also made its eyes, but the smile was missing. They decided to go into the house, even though they hadn't finished the snowman yet.

"Where's Tim?" he asked Mom, as soon as he saw her in the kitchen doing the dishes.

"I think he has the flu, Danny! He has a fever and has gone to bed. That's a shame, isn't it?"

"I know why he got sick." Jeremy shouted at Liddy and Daniel.

Daniel felt very bad. He saw them from his window and he saw the way they were looking at each other. They had been outside for several hours.

They went upstairs and went to Tim's bedroom.

"How are you feeling?" Daniel asked. But Tim was almost asleep.

"I'll be fine as soon as she comes back to me...," he murmured, and rolled over again.

"Forget Liddy. Tim is love-sick!" Daniel thought to himself.

It had been a very cold week.

Danny didn't go downstairs to say good-bye to the Pattersons
that night. He went to his bedroom and stayed there until
his American parents came to say good-night.

He pretended to be asleep. His eyes were burning and he was sneezing.

Some classmates from school came over to visit them
in their bedrooms. Daniel had caught a cold and his
brother was even worse. Tim had the measles.

"There's a very special guest for you here, Danny," Mom said as she
opened the door to his room on that December twenty-sixth.

"Can I come in?" It was Liddy, and she looked wonderful.

"Go slow, Daniel!" He thought.

"I'm sorry about your cold. It was probably the snow the other day,"
she said, and gave him some newspapers with news about Brazil.

"Oh, that's terrific," he said. He was delighted.

They heard Tim saying "Liddy, are you there?"

Poor sick brothers, suffering over the love for the same girl.

"Yes, Tim. I'm coming!" She looked at Daniel and left his bedroom.

There was another patient waiting for her care.

Daniel wanted to go to Tim's bedroom to hear what they were talking about but he couldn't. Jeremy wanted his attention.

Liddy went out but left an invitation to the party next to his bed:

Are you coming to our party or not?

I'm counting on your being there.

Finally he decided to talk to Tim. He would tell him about Liddy, about his feelings.

"Tim? Are you taking a shower?" Daniel asked him.

"Yes. I'm almost finished," Tim answered.

He sat on Tim's bed and then saw Liddy's picture on the bedside table. She was kissing Tim on the cheek. He turned it over, and on the back it read:

"Tim, I'll always love you."

"I want to go to Liddy's party with you," Tim said as he opened the door.

"How come, Tim? You're sicker than I am."

"You'll help me, won't you?"

Daniel was worried about his American parents. They hadn't let him go to the party because he would give his cold to everybody else.

He knew he wanted to go because of Liddy and he decided to help his brother out.

Their parents had taken Jeremy to the movies and had asked Daniel to give Tim his medicine.

As soon as they left, Tim and Daniel ran and got dressed and went over to Liddy's party.

A girl named Sue opened the front door. "Liddy," she shouted. "Come here! It's Danny, your friend from Brazil!"

"Hi! I'm glad you're here Daniel. Hi, Tim! Are you feeling better?" she asked.

"She looks beautiful in that red skirt and yellow pullover," Daniel thought.

There was a D.J, lots of other kids and a lot of potato chips and dip and soft drinks.

Everybody was very nice and tried to make Daniel feel at home.

Tim and Liddy had disappeared and Daniel felt very uncomfortable about that.

He was thirsty so he went to the kitchen to get something to drink. He was shocked when he saw Tim kissing Liddy right before his eyes. They must have made up again.

Daniel went back into the living-room and he decided he wouldn't spoil everything for them.

Then a girl named Sylvia came over and invited Daniel to dance. It was very nice of Tom, the D.J., to play some Brazilian songs. They were already dancing when Liddy stopped in front of them and said:

"Shall we dance now, Danny?"

Sylvia left and Liddy put her arms around Daniel's neck.

He couldn't figure out what was going on. She was kissing his "brother" a few minutes ago and now she wanted to dance with him.

"Listen, I saw you and Tim in the kitchen. I won't get you into trouble," he started to say. But suddenly he was seeing double.

"Who was that other 'Liddy' sitting on the stairs with Tim?" Daniel wondered.

He was so pale that Liddy stopped dancing and looked too.

"Wait!" she said. "Didn't anybody tell you I have a twin sister?" She started laughing. "That's Lilly! She just came in from Nashville!" She pointed at a girl that looked exactly like her. "She couldn't come for Christmas because she was at Grandma's farm. There was so much snow that she had to stay there until…" Daniel wasn't able to pay attention to the rest of the explanation.

"Liddy and Lilly?" Daniel was very, very surprised.

"Yes! She broke up with Tim a month ago and I was trying to help him...," she started to explain.

No further explanations were needed. Daniel wanted to dance with Liddy, to know her better and to relax. He deserved it.

Later she introduced him to her twin sister. Lilly was wearing a red skirt and a yellow pullover too. Then he noticed she had a birthmark on her left cheek. That was the only difference between them.

"Man, I feel a lot better, now," Tim whispered. "You're a lucky guy! Liddy has a bit of a temper but Lilly..., she drives me crazy! Look at the ring I gave her," pointing at the girl's finger. "That was my surprise! I hope she has forgiven me by now... I was dating two girls at the same time." he confessed.

Then Daniel realized his Mom had tried to say something about the twin when she introduced him to Liddy's family on Christmas Eve but he had interrupted her at the time.

The boys didn't think their parents would find out about the party, but they were wrong. Lilly got the measles from Tim.

Now Liddy and Daniel are dating. She's interested in Brazil, and she helps him with his homework and corrects his English. She's also teaching him how to dance. Daniel has taught her some words in Portuguese and gave her a Brazilian ring with a pretty stone in it.

A journalist went to their school yesterday morning. It was February 14th, Valentine's Day. Tim explained to Daniel that Americans give their girlfriends and boyfriends chocolates in heart-shaped boxes. It's different from Brazil.

So the journalist had come to their school to interview boys and girls about Valentine's day.

Look at their picture in the paper. Isn't that cool?

THE AUTHOR

My name is Telma Guimarães. I was born in Marília, São Paulo. When I was a teenager, I took an Exchange program in Covington, Georgia. It was a wonderful experience. I graduated with a bachelor degree in Languages, English and Literature at UNESP. I moved to Campinas and then I started teaching English. I have three children and I loved telling stories to my kids. Many of the stories were created by me.

My heart was always full of joy when I sat on my chair and thought about children, animals, nature and so on. So, I gave up teaching and tried to reach my goal: to be an author. Here I am!

Quadro Europeu Comum de
Referência para Línguas (CEFR)

A1

A2

B1

B2

C1

C2

The brazilian exchange student
© 2022 by Telma Guimarães

Presidência Mario Ghio Júnior
Vice-presidência de educação digital Camila Montero Vaz Cardoso
Direção editorial Lidiane Vivaldini Olo
Gerência editorial Julio Cesar Augustus de Paula Santos
Coordenação editorial Laura Vecchioli do Prado
Aprendizagem digital Renata Galdino (ger.), Beatriz de Almeida Pinto Rodrigues da Costa (coord. Experiência de Aprendizagem), Carla Isabel Ferreira Reis (coord. Produção Multimídia), Daniella dos Santos Di Nubila (coord. Produção Digital), Rogerio Fabio Alves (coord. Publicação), Vanessa Tavares Menezes de Souza (coord. Design Digital)
Planejamento, controle de produção e indicadores Flávio Matuguma (ger.), Juliana Batista (coord.) e Jayne Ruas (analista)
Edição Instituto Parole
Revisão Ray Shoulder e Maria Claudia Franchi
Projeto gráfico e diagramação Estúdio Kiwi - Thiago Lopes
Ilustração Estúdio Kiwi - Eduardo Ramuski
Capa Thatiana Kalaes

Dados Internacionais de Catalogação na Publicação (CIP)

Guimarães, Telma
    The brazilian exchange student / Telma Guimarães ; ilustrações de Estúdio Kiwi. -- São Paulo : Saraiva, 2022.
    40 p. : il.

IISBN 978-65-5867-115-2

1. Literatura infantojuvenil - Língua inglesa (Ensino Fundamental) I. Título II. Estúdio Kiwi

22-4988   CDD 428.24

Angélica Ilacqua CRB-8/7057

CL: 531272
CAE: 795110

2022
1ª edição
1ª tiragem
Impressão e acabamento: Gráfica Elyon

Direitos desta edição cedidos à Somos Sistemas de Ensino S.A.
Av. Paulista, 901, Bela Vista – São Paulo – SP – CEP 01310-200
Tel.: (0xx11) 4003-3061
Conheça o nosso portal de literatura Coletivo Leitor: www.coletivoleitor.com.br

Este livro foi composto na fonte **Aleo** e
impresso sobre papel off set 90 g/m2.